Piano · Vocal · Guitar

THE ANIMATION COLLECTION

ISBN 978-1-4234-9228-3

HAL•LEONARD®
CORPORATION
7777 W. BLUEMOUND RD. P.O. BOX 13819 MILWAUKEE, WI 53213

Visit Hal Leonard Online at
www.halleonard.com

CONTENTS

ACCIDENTALLY IN LOVE

from the Motion Picture SHREK 2

Words and Music by ADAM F. DURITZ,
DAN VICKREY, DAVID IMMERGLUCK,
MATTHEW MALLEY and DAVID BRYSON

So she said, _"What's the prob-lem, ba - by?"_ What's the prob-lem? I don't know. Well, may-be I'm in love (love). Think a - bout it, ev - 'ry time I think a - bout it,

BLAME CANADA

from the Motion Picture Soundtrack SOUTH PARK: BIGGER, LONGER & UNCUT

Words and Music by TREY PARKER
and MARC SHAIMAN

stead, he burned up like a pig-gy on a bar-be-cue.

Men: Should we blame the match-es? Should we blame the

fire, or the doc-tors who al-lowed him to ex-

pire? *Kyle's Mom:* Heck, no! *All:* Blame Can-a-da,

Ain't No Mountain High Enough

featured in Walt Disney's CHICKEN LITTLE

Words and Music by NICKOLAS ASHFORD
and VALERIE SIMPSON

(Spoken:) If you need me, call me;

no matter where you are, no matter how far. Just call my name,

I'll be there in a hurry. On that you can depend and never worry.

(No wind, __

No wind, __ no rain, __ or win-ter's cold __

__ no rain _____ or win-ter's cold __

ALMOST THERE

from Walt Disney's THE PRINCESS AND THE FROG

Music and Lyrics by
RANDY NEWMAN

Moderately, expressively

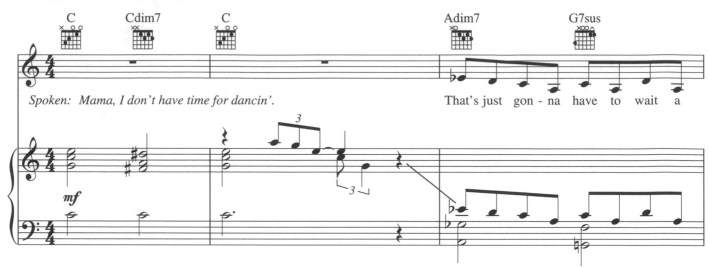

Spoken: Mama, I don't have time for dancin'.

That's just gon-na have to wait a

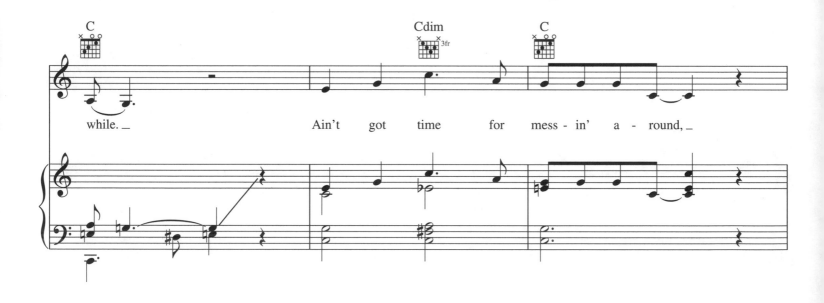

while. _ Ain't got time for mess-in' a-round, _

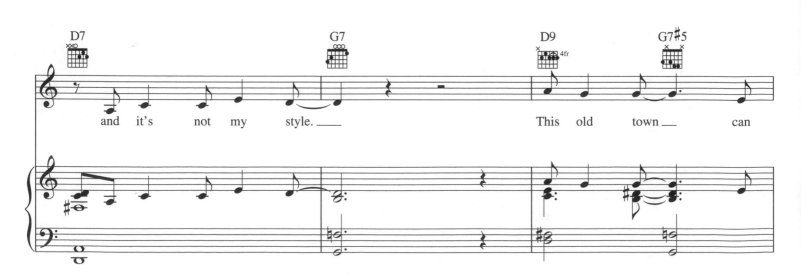

and it's not my style. ____ This old town ___ can

THE BARE NECESSITIES

from Walt Disney's THE JUNGLE BOOK

Words and Music by
TERRY GILKYSON

(Mowgli & Baloo:) Look for the bare ne - ces - si - ties, __ the
(2.) Tuba solo

sim - ple, bare ne - ces - si - ties. __ For - get a - bout __ your

wor - ries and your strife. I mean the

To Coda ⊕

fond - er ____ of my big home.
raw paw, __ well, next time, be - ware.

Baloo: The bees are buzz - ing in the tree ____ to make some

hon - ey, just __ for me. When you look un - der the

rocks and plants, _ take a glance at the fan - cy ants __ and

CODA

Don't pick the prick-ly pear __ by the paw; when you pick a pear, __ try to use the claw, __ but you don't need to use the claw __ when you pick a pear of the big paw - paw.

(Spoken:) Have I given you a clue?

BEAUTY AND THE BEAST

from Walt Disney's BEAUTY AND THE BEAST

Lyrics by HOWARD ASHMAN
Music by ALAN MENKEN

BEYOND THE SEA

featured in the Walt Disney/Pixar film FINDING NEMO

Lyrics by JACK LAWRENCE
Music by CHARLES TRENET and ALBERT LASRY
Original French Lyric to "La Mer" by
CHARLES TRENET

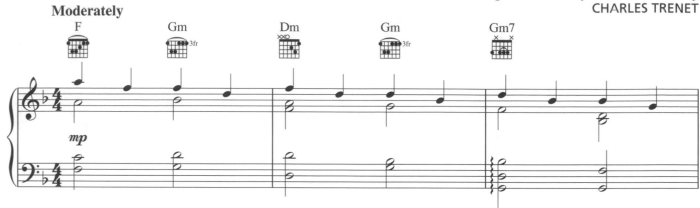

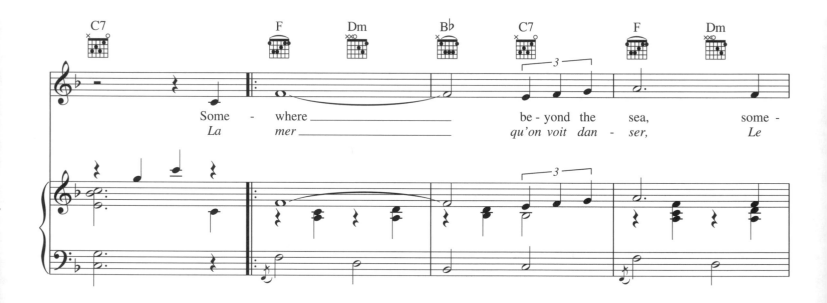

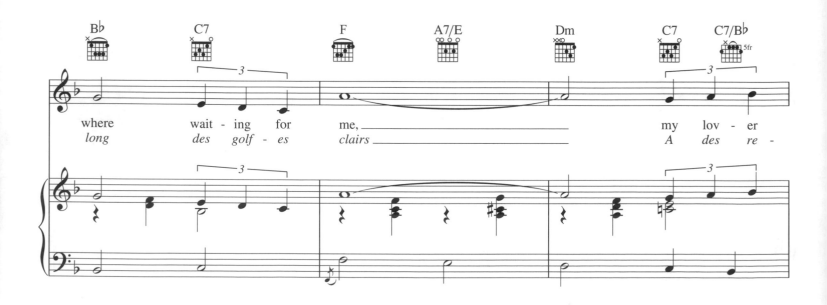

BIBBIDI-BOBBIDI-BOO
(The Magic Song)
from Walt Disney's CINDERELLA

Words by JERRY LIVINGSTON
Music by MACK DAVID and AL HOFFMAN

Brightly

Sa-la-ga-doo-la men-chic-ka boo-la

bib-bi-di-bob-bi-di-boo. Put 'em to-geth-er and what have you got bib-bi-di-bob-bi-di-boo.

Sa-la-ga-doo-la men-chic-ka boo-la bib-bi-di-bob-bi-di-boo. It-'ll do mag-ic be-lieve it or not,

CAN YOU FEEL THE LOVE TONIGHT

from Walt Disney Pictures' THE LION KING

Music by ELTON JOHN
Lyrics by TIM RICE

There's a calm __ sur-ren - der
There's a time __ for ev-'ry - one,

to the rush __ of day, __ when the heat __ of the roll-ing world __
if they on - ly learn __ that the twist - ing ka-lei-do-scope __

can be turned __ a - way. __ An en-chant - ed mo-ment,
moves us all __ in turn. __ There's a rhyme __ and rea - son

CAR WASH
featured in SHARK TALE

Words and Music by
NORMAN WHITFIELD

Moderately slow (with a double time feel)

Clap hands

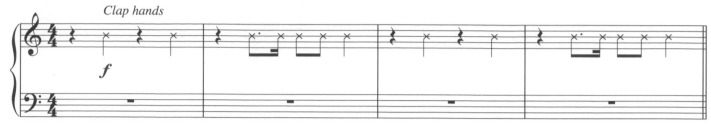

Woo _____

You might not ev - er get

rich

but let me tell ya it's bet - ter than dig - gin' a ditch. _

To Coda ⊕

Come on and sing it with me car wash. __

Get with the feel - in' y'all __ car wash __ yeah. __

N.C.

1

Come sum-mer the work gets kind - a hard. __

This ain't no place to be if ya

planned on be - ing a star. ___ Let me tell you it's al - ways

cool, and the boss don't mind some - times if ya

act a fool. ___ At the well, those

(Work and work)

cars nev - er seem to stop com - in'. keep ___

(Work and work)

chines ____ hum - min'. Let me tell you it's al - ways

cool, and the boss don't mind some - times if you

act a fool at the car wash. __

Repeat and Fade

{ Work - in' at the } car wash, __ yeah! __
{ Talk - in' a - bout the }

THE CHICKEN DANCE

featured in JIMMY NEUTRON: BOY GENIUS

By TERRY RENDALL
and WERNER THOMAS
English Lyrics by PAUL PARNES

Additional Lyrics

2. Hey, you're in the swing.
   You're cluckin' like a bird. (Pluck, pluck, pluck, pluck.)
   You're flappin' your wings.
   Don't you feel absurd. (No, no, no, no.)
   It's a chicken dance,
   Like a rooster and a hen. (Ya, ya, ya, ya.)
   Flappy chicken dance;
   Let's do it again. *(To Chorus 2:)*

   Chorus 2:
   Relax and let the music move you.
   Let all your inhibitions go.
   Just watch your partner whirl around you.
   We're havin' fun now; I told you so.

3. Now you're flappin' like a bird
   And you're wigglin' too. (I like that move.)
   You're without a care.
   It's a dance for you. (Just made for you.)
   Keep doin' what you do.
   Don't you cop out now. (Don't cop out now.)
   Gets better as you dance;
   Catch your breath somehow.
   Chorus

4. Now we're almost through,
   Really flyin' high. (Bye, bye, bye, bye.)
   All you chickens and birds,
   Time to say goodbye. (To say goodbye.)
   Goin' back to the nest,
   But the flyin' was fun. (Oh, it was fun.)
   Chicken dance was the best,
   But the dance is done.

CASPER THE FRIENDLY GHOST

from the Paramount Cartoon

Words by MACK DAVID
Music by JERRY LIVINGSTON

CIRCLE OF LIFE
from Walt Disney Pictures' THE LION KING

Music by ELTON JOHN
Lyrics by TIM RICE

70

cir - cle, _____ the cir - cle ___ of life,

COLORS OF THE WIND
(Pop Version)

from Walt Disney's POCAHONTAS
as performed by Vanessa Williams

Music by ALAN MENKEN
Lyrics by STEPHEN SCHWARTZ

D.S. al Coda

Lyrics:

skinned, we need to sing with all __ the voic-es __ of the moun-tain, we need to

paint with all __ the col-ors of the wind. You can own the earth __ and still all you'll

own is earth un-til you can paint with all the col-ors of the wind.

DO IT AGAIN

featured in HAPPY FEET

Words and Music by BRIAN WILSON
and MIKE LOVE

With a solid beat

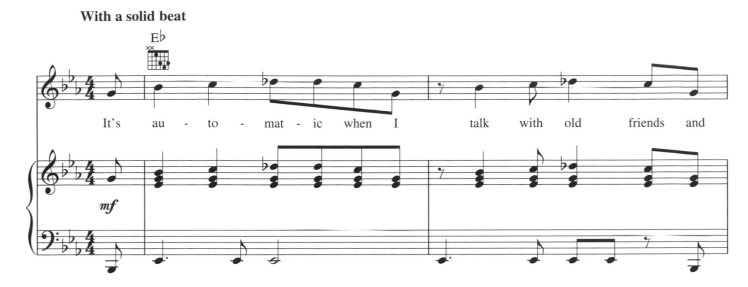

A DREAM IS A WISH YOUR HEART MAKES

from Walt Disney's CINDERELLA

Words and Music by MACK DAVID,
AL HOFFMAN and JERRY LIVINGSTON

When I was a lit-tle { girl, } { boy, } my fa-ther used to say, if trou-ble ev-er trou-bles you, just dream your cares a-way. A dream is a wish your heart makes ____

ELEANOR RIGBY

from YELLOW SUBMARINE

Words and Music by JOHN LENNON
and PAUL McCARTNEY

Moderately, with a steady beat

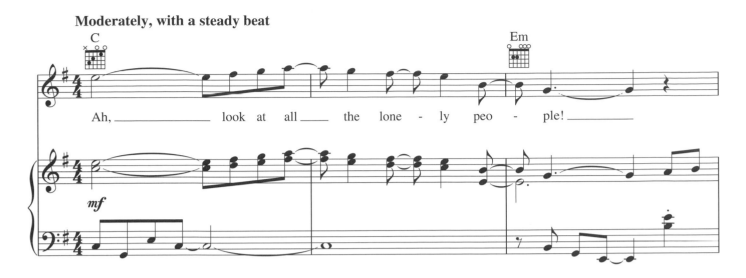

Ah, _____ look at all ___ the lone - ly peo - ple! _____

Ah, _____ look at all ___ the lone - ly peo -

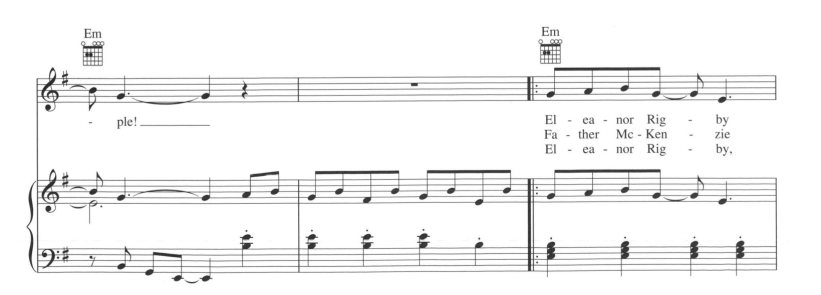

- ple! _____

El - ea - nor Rig - by
Fa - ther Mc - Ken - zie
El - ea - nor Rig - by,

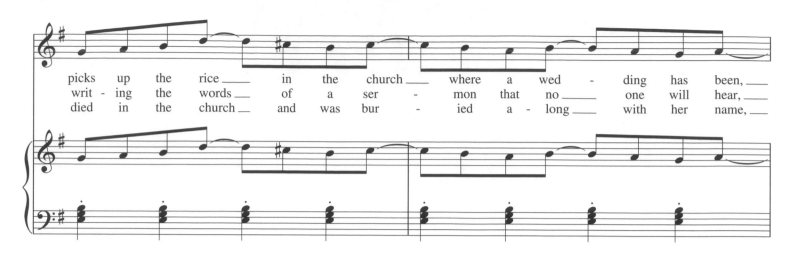

picks up the rice ____ in the church ____ where a wed - ding has been, ____
writ - ing the words ____ of a ser - mon that no ____ one will hear, ____
died in the church ____ and was bur - ied a - long ____ with her name, ____

____ Lives in a dream. _____ Waits at the win - dow,
____ No one comes near. _____ Look at him work - ing,
____ No - bod - y came. _____ Fa - ther Mc - Ken - zie,

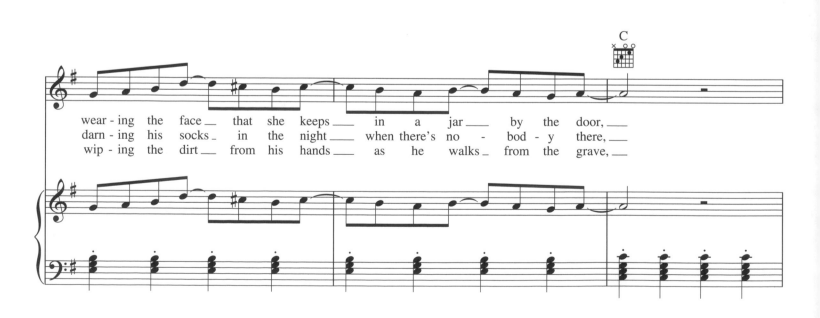

wear - ing the face ____ that she keeps ____ in a jar ____ by the door, ____
darn - ing his socks ____ in the night ____ when there's no - bod - y there, ____
wip - ing the dirt ____ from his hands ____ as he walks ____ from the grave, ____

THEME FROM FAMILY GUY

from the Twentieth Century Fox Television Series FAMILY GUY

Words by SETH MacFARLANE and DAVID ZUCKERMAN
Music by WALTER MURPHY

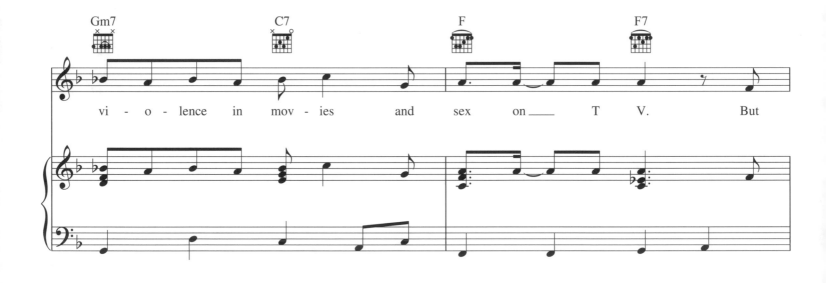

It seems to-day ___ that all you see ___ is

vi - o - lence in mov - ies and sex on ___ T. V. But

where are those good old - fash - ioned ___ val - ues

GIVE A LITTLE WHISTLE
from Walt Disney's PINOCCHIO

Words by NED WASHINGTON
Music by LEIGH HARLINE

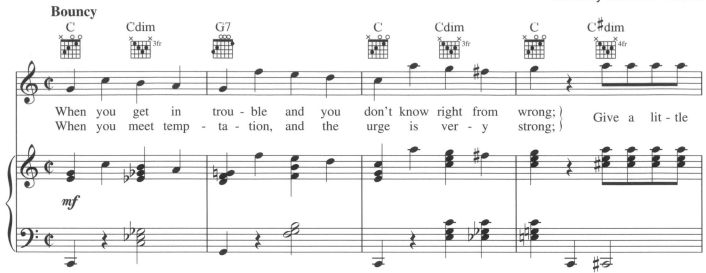

When you get in trou-ble and you don't know right from wrong;
When you meet temp-ta-tion, and the urge is ver-y strong; } Give a lit-tle

whis-tle! (Whistle _____) Give a lit-tle whis-tle! (Whistle _____)

_____) Not just a lit-tle squeak; Puck-er up and

GO THE DISTANCE
from Walt Disney Pictures' HERCULES

Music by ALAN MENKEN
Lyrics by DAVID ZIPPEL

I have of-ten dreamed of a far-off place where a he-ro's wel-come would be wait-ing for me, where the crowds will cheer when they

un-known road to em-brace my fate, a though that road may wan-der, it will lead me to you. And a thou-sand years would be

I'M POPEYE THE SAILOR MAN

Theme from the Paramount Cartoon POPEYE THE SAILOR

Words and Music by
SAMMY LERNER

GOD HELP THE OUTCASTS

from Walt Disney's THE HUNCHBACK OF NOTRE DAME

Music by ALAN MENKEN
Lyrics by STEPHEN SCHWARTZ

HALLELUJAH

featured in the DreamWorks Motion Picture SHREK

Words and Music by
LEONARD COHEN

Moderately slow, in 2

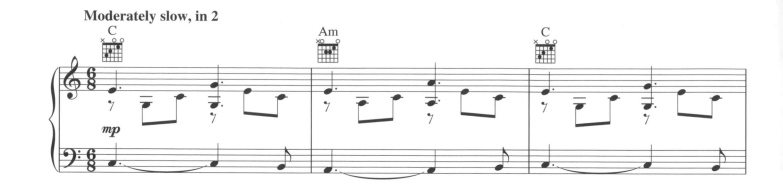

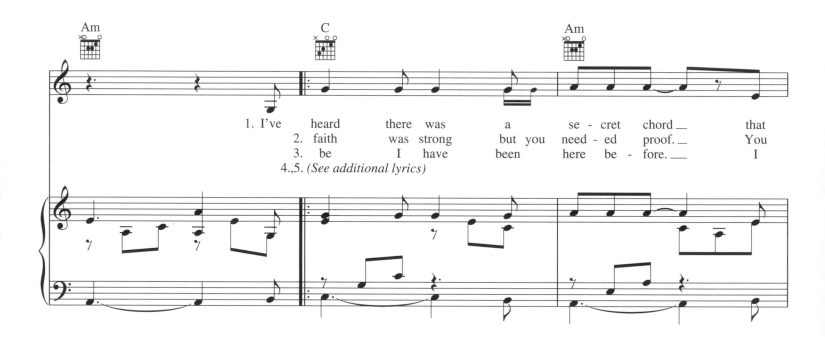

1. I've heard there was a se - cret chord ___ that
2. faith was strong but you need - ed proof. ___ You
3. be I have been here be - fore. ___ I
4.,5. *(See additional lyrics)*

Da - vid played, ___ and it pleased the Lord, ___ but you don't ___ real - ly
saw ___ her ___ bath - ing on the roof. ___ Her beau - ty ___ and the
know this room; ___ I've ___ walked this floor. ___ I used to ___ live a -

Chorus

lu - jah. _____ Hal - le - lu - jah. _____ Hal - le -

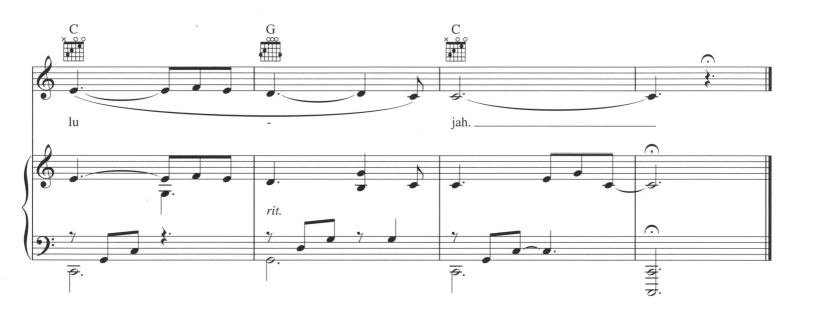

lu - jah. _____

Additional Lyrics

4. There was a time you let me know
   What's real and going on below.
   But now you never show it to me, do you?
   And remember when I moved in you.
   The holy dark was movin', too,
   And every breath we drew was Hallelujah.
   Chorus

5. Maybe there's a God above,
   And all I ever learned from love
   Was how to shoot at someone who outdrew you.
   And it's not a cry you can hear at night.
   It's not somebody who's seen the light.
   It's a cold and it's a broken Hallelujah.
   Chorus

HAWAIIAN ROLLER COASTER RIDE

from Walt Disney's LILO & STITCH

Words and Music by ALAN SILVESTRI
and MARK KEALI'I HO'OMALU

1.,3. *Lead:* There's   no ___ place I'd rath - er be ___ *Chorus:* than on   my surf - board out   at   sea.
2. *All:* There's   no ___ place I'd rath - er be ___ *Chorus:* than on   the sea - shore dry, wet,   free.

*Children's Chorus

Lead: lin - ger - ing ___ in the o - cean blue. ___ *Chorus:* And if   I   had   one   wish come   true *Lead:* I'd
All: On   gold - en sand is ___ where I'd ___ lay, *Chorus:* and if   I   on - ly   had   my   way *All:* I'd

116

HEIGH-HO
The Dwarfs' Marching Song from Walt Disney's
SNOW WHITE AND THE SEVEN DWARFS

Words by LARRY MOREY
Music by FRANK CHURCHILL

Bright and cheerful

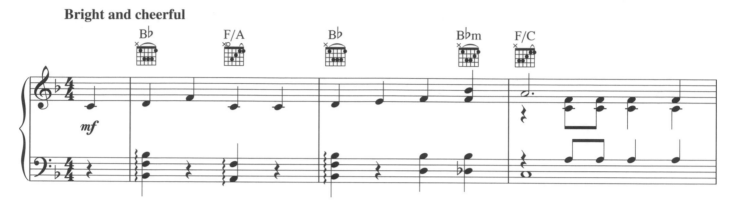

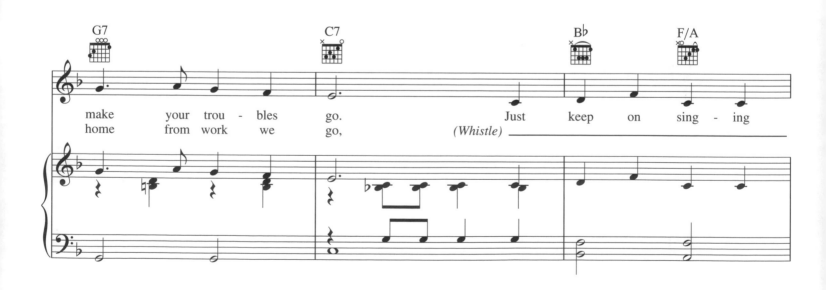

I'M LATE

from Walt Disney's ALICE IN WONDERLAND

Words by BOB HILLIARD
Music by SAMMY FAIN

Brightly

I'm late, I'm late for a ver-y im-por-tant date. No

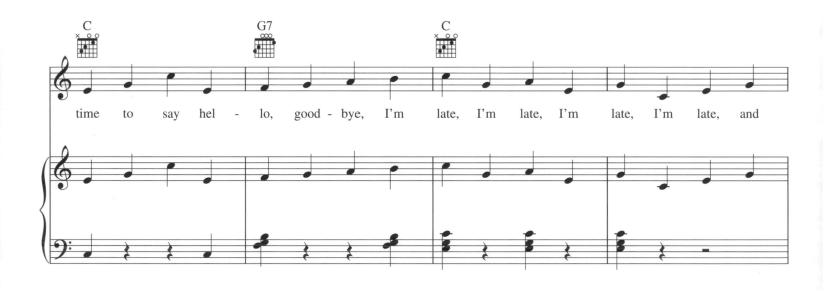

time to say hel - lo, good-bye, I'm late, I'm late, I'm late, I'm late, and

when I wave, I lose the time I save. My fuzz - y ears and

IF I DIDN'T HAVE YOU

Walt Disney Pictures Presents A Pixar Animation Studios Film MONSTERS, INC.

Music and Lyrics by
RANDY NEWMAN

ICE AGE - SCORE

from ICE AGE

Composed by
DAVID NEWMAN

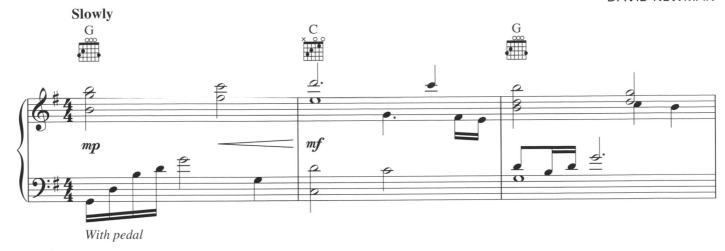

Slowly

With pedal

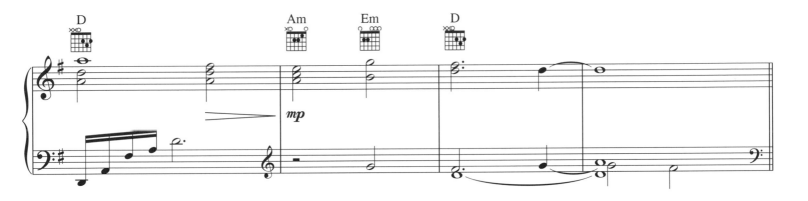

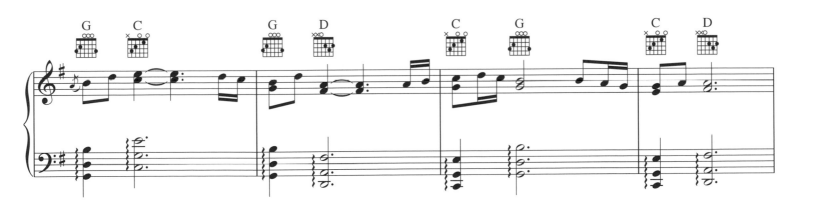

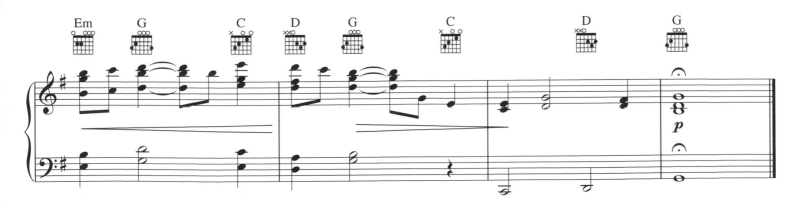

THE INCREDITS

from Walt Disney Pictures' THE INCREDIBLES – A Pixar Film

Music by MICHAEL GIACCHINO

Sax solo ad lib.

Sax solo ends

JOURNEY TO THE PAST

from the Twentieth Century Fox Motion Picture ANASTASIA

Words and Music by LYNN AHRENS
and STEPHEN FLAHERTY

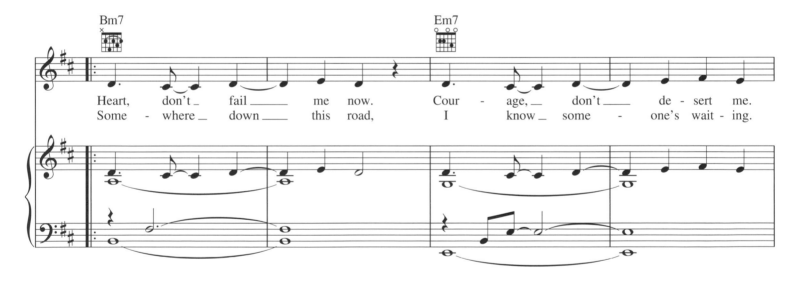

Heart, don't fail me now. Courage, don't desert me.
Some- where down this road, I know some- one's wait- ing.

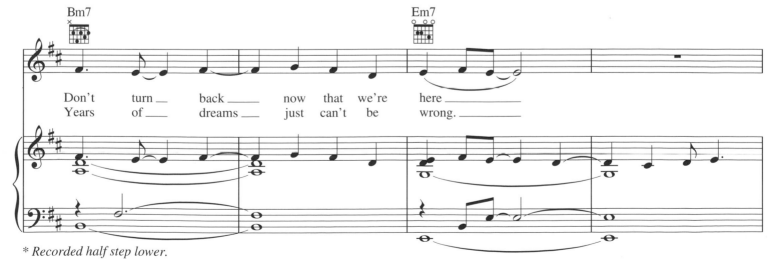

Don't turn back now that we're here
Years of dreams just can't be wrong.

* *Recorded half step lower.*

THEME FROM KING OF THE HILL

from the Twentieth Century Fox Television Series KING OF THE HILL

By ROGER CLYNE, BRIAN BLUSH,
ARTHUR EDWARDS and PAUL NAFFAH

KISS THE GIRL

from Walt Disney's THE LITTLE MERMAID

Lyrics by HOWARD ASHMAN
Music by ALAN MENKEN

Now's your mo-ment, _____ float-ing in a blue la-goon. _____

LIFE IS A HIGHWAY

featured in Walt Disney Pictures' CARS - A Pixar Film

Words and Music by
TOM COCHRANE

Life's like a road ___ that you trav-el on when there's one ___ day here ___ and the next ___ day gone. ___ Some-times ___
all these cit-ies and all these towns, it's in my blood ___ and it's all ___ a-round. ___ I love ___

LOOK THROUGH MY EYES

from Walt Disney Pictures' BROTHER BEAR

Words and Music by
PHIL COLLINS

*Recorded a whole step higher.

LINUS AND LUCY
from A BOY NAMED CHARLIE BROWN

By VINCE GUARALDI

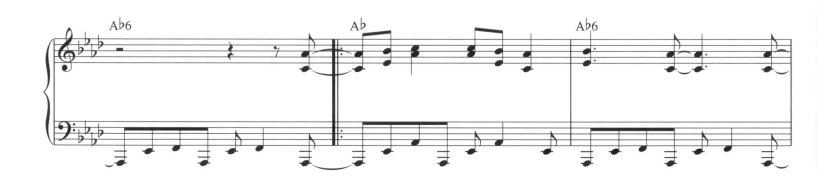

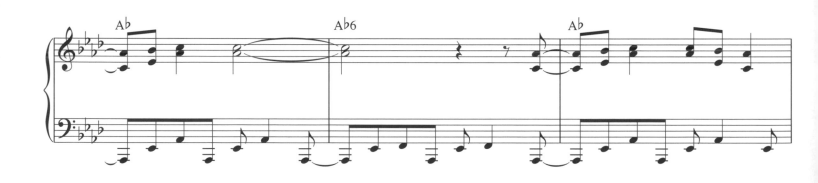

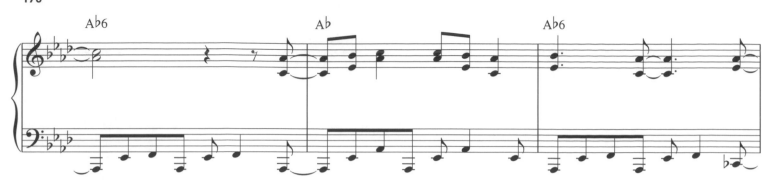

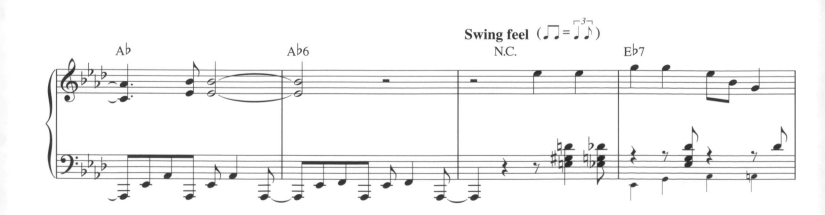

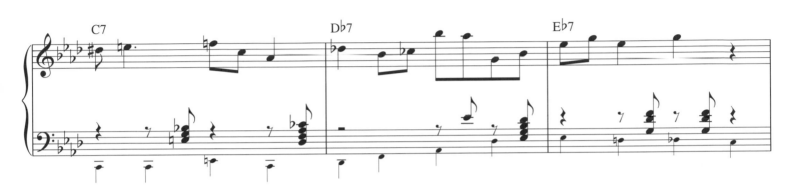

ONCE UPON A DREAM
from Walt Disney's SLEEPING BEAUTY

Words and Music by SAMMY FAIN
and JACK LAWRENCE
Adapted from a Theme by TCHAIKOVSKY

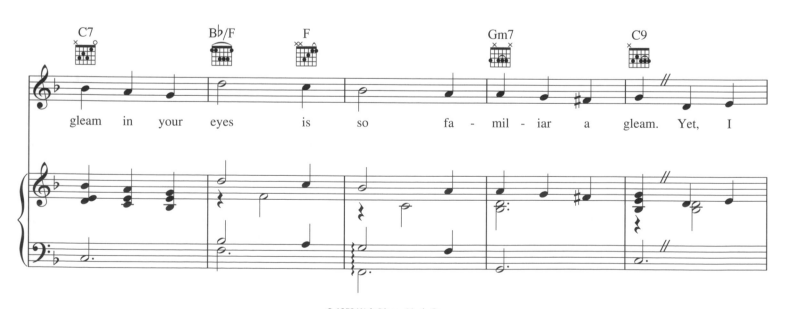

REFLECTION
from Walt Disney Pictures' MULAN

Music by MATTHEW WILDER
Lyrics by DAVID ZIPPEL

Look at me, you may think you see who I really am, but you'll never know me. Ev-'ry day it's as if I play a part.

SOMEWHERE OUT THERE
from AN AMERICAN TAIL

Music by BARRY MANN and JAMES HORNER
Lyric by CYNTHIA WEIL

through, then we'll be to-geth - er some-where out there, out

where dreams come true. _____

ROCKY & BULLWINKLE
from the Cartoon Television Series

By FRANK COMSTOCK

THEME FROM THE SIMPSONS™

from THE SIMPSONS

Music by DANNY ELFMAN

Moderately fast

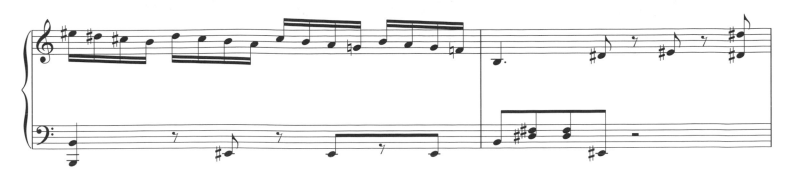

SOME DAY MY PRINCE WILL COME

from Walt Disney's SNOW WHITE AND THE SEVEN DWARFS

Words by LARRY MOREY
Music by FRANK CHURCHILL

Some day my prince will come, Some
Some day I'll find my love, Some -

day I'll find my love, and how thrill - ing that
one to call my own, and I'll know her the

mo - ment will be, _____ When the prince of my dreams comes to
mo - ment we meet, _____ For my heart will start skip - ping a

8vb

SOMEDAY OUT OF THE BLUE
(Theme from El Dorado)
from THE ROAD TO EL DORADO

Music by ELTON JOHN and PATRICK LEONARD
Lyrics by TIM RICE

Some - day out of the blue, ___ in a crowd - ed street or a de - sert - ed square, ___ I'll turn and I'll ___ see ___ you, as if our love ___ were

SPIDER PIG
from THE SIMPSONS MOVIE

Based on the composition "Theme from Spiderman"
written by PAUL FRANCIS WEBSTER and BOB HARRIS
Parody Lyrics by JAMES I. BROOKS,
MATT GROENING, AL JEAN, IAN MAXTONE GRAHAM,
GEORGE MEYER, DAVID MIRKIN, MIKE REISS,
MIKE SCULLY, MATT SELMAN,
JOHN SWARTZWELDER and JON VITTI

SPONGEBOB SQUAREPANTS THEME SONG

from SPONGEBOB SQUAREPANTS

Words and Music by MARK HARRISON,
BLAISE SMITH, STEVE HILLENBURG
and DEREK DRYMON

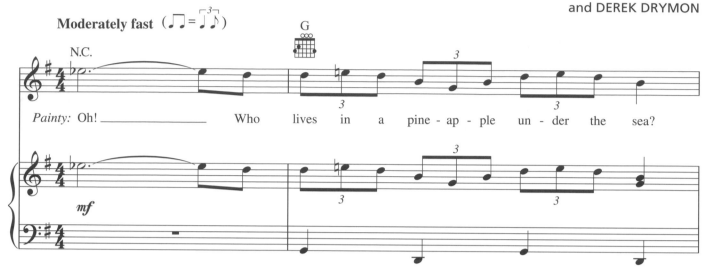

Painty: Oh! _____ Who lives in a pine-ap-ple un-der the sea?

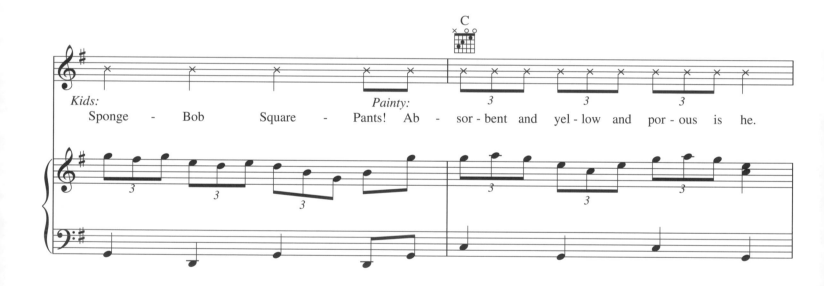

Kids: Sponge - Bob Square - Pants! Painty: Ab - sor-bent and yel-low and por-ous is he.

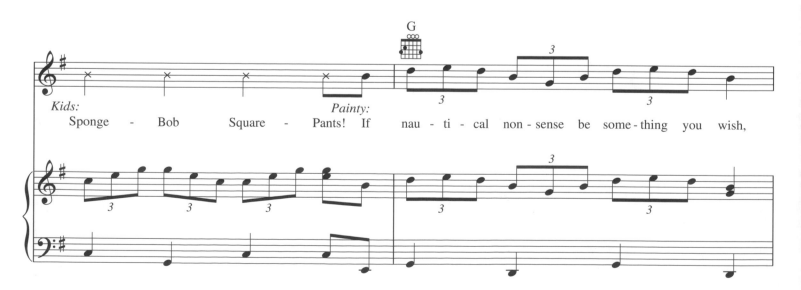

Kids: Sponge - Bob Square - Pants! Painty: If nau-ti-cal non-sense be some-thing you wish,

STAYIN' ALIVE
featured in MADAGASCAR

Words and Music by BARRY GIBB,
ROBIN GIBB and MAURICE GIBB

WHEN YOU BELIEVE
(From THE PRINCE OF EGYPT)

Words and Music by STEPHEN SCHWARTZ
with Additional Music by BABYFACE

Many nights we've prayed, with no proof an-y-one could hear.

In our hearts a hope-ful song we bare-ly un-der-stood. Now

we are not a-fraid, al-though we know there's much to fear.

nev - er thought I'd say: ___ There can be mir - a - cles, ___

when you be - lieve. ___ Though hope is frail, it's hard to kill.
(When you be - lieve.)

Who knows what mir - a - cles ___ you ___ can a - chieve? ___
(You can a -

When you be - lieve, ___ some - how ___ you will. ___
chieve?)

THIS IS HALLOWEEN
from Tim Burton's THE NIGHTMARE BEFORE CHRISTMAS

Music and Lyrics by
DANNY ELFMAN

THIS IS IT
Theme from THE BUGS BUNNY SHOW

Words and Music by MACK DAVID
and JERRY LIVINGSTON

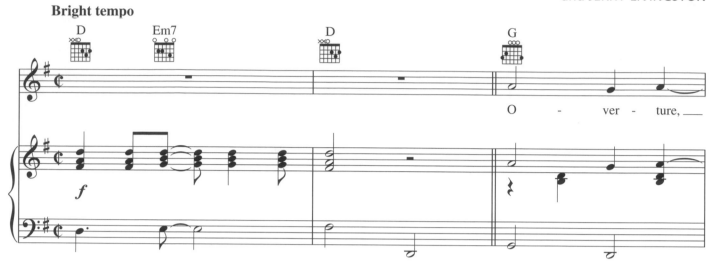

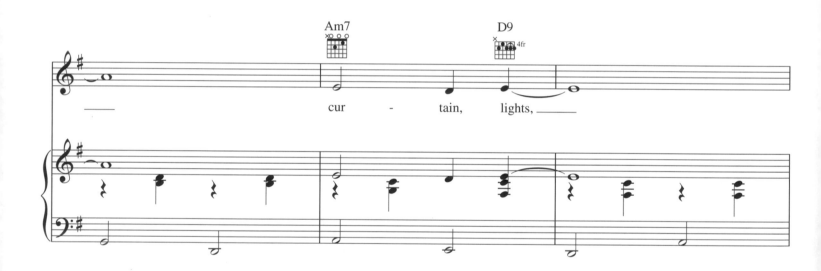

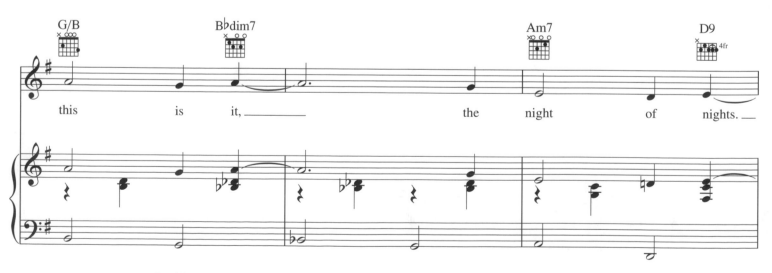

UNDER THE SEA
from Walt Disney's THE LITTLE MERMAID

Music by ALAN MENKEN
Lyrics by HOWARD ASHMAN

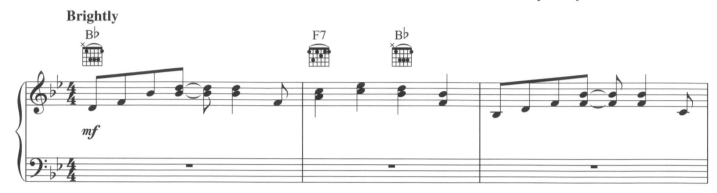

The sea-weed is al-ways green-er
Down here __ all the fish is hap-py

in some-bod-y else-'s lake.
as off __ through the waves dey roll.

You dream __ a-bout
The fish __ on the

oh,   that blow - fish   blow.

Un-der the sea.   Un - der the sea.

When _ the sar - dine be - gin _ the be - guine, it's mu - sic to

WALLACE & GROMIT THEME
from WALLACE AND GROMIT

By JULIAN NOTT

March-like

WALTZ OF THE FLOWERS

featured in Walt Disney's FANTASIA

By PYOTR IL'YICH TCHAIKOVSKY

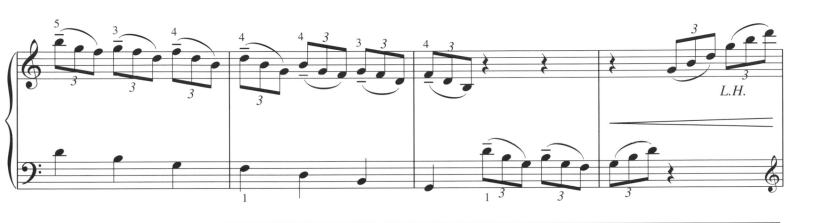

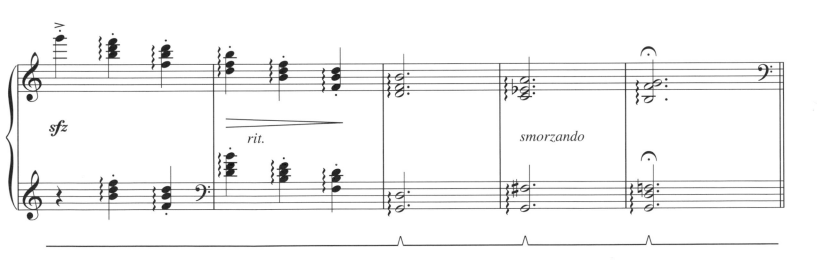

WE ARE THE CHAMPIONS

featured in Walt Disney's CHICKEN LITTLE

Words and Music by
FREDDIE MERCURY

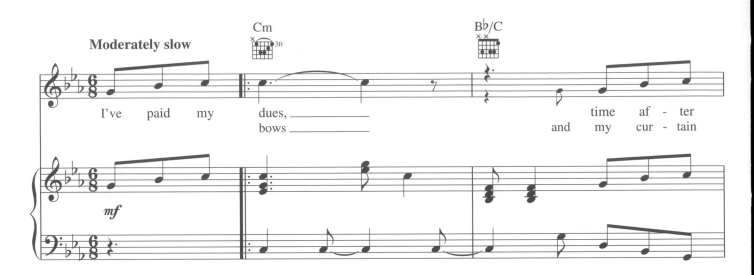

I've paid my dues, _____ time af- ter
bows _____ and my cur- tain

time.
calls.

I've done my _____ sen- tence
You brought me _____ fame and for- tune and ev- 'ry- thing that

goes with it,
but com- mit- ted no _____ crime.
I thank you all. _____

WHAT A WONDERFUL WORLD
featured in MADAGASCAR

Words and Music by GEORGE DAVID WEISS
and BOB THIELE

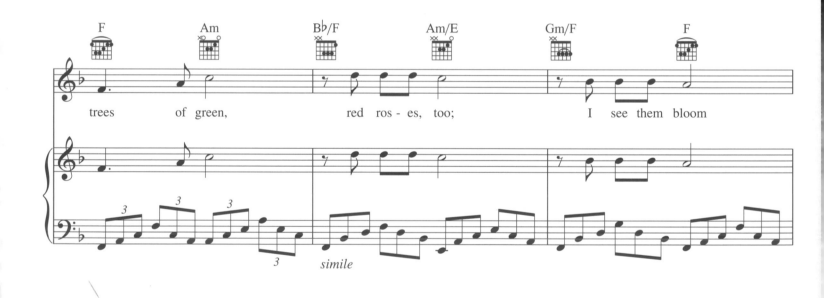

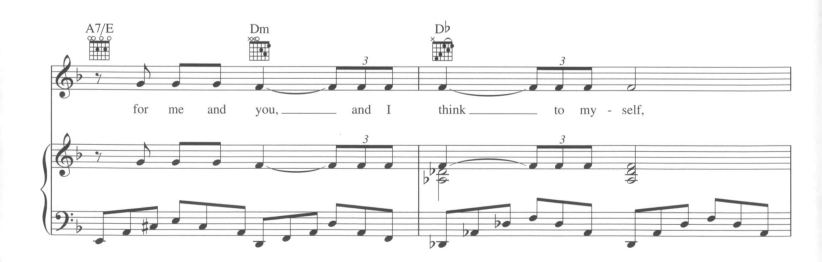

WHEN SHE LOVED ME

from Walt Disney Pictures' TOY STORY 2 - A Pixar Film

Music and Lyrics by
RANDY NEWMAN

Tenderly, very freely

When some - bod - y loved me, ev - 'ry-thing was beau-ti - ful.

Ev - 'ry hour we spent to-geth - er lives with-in my heart. And when she was sad,

I was there to dry her tears; and when she was hap - py, so was I, when

WHEN YOU WISH UPON A STAR

from Walt Disney's PINOCCHIO

Words by NED WASHINGTON
Music by LEIGH HARLINE

WHO'S AFRAID OF THE BIG BAD WOLF?

from Walt Disney's THREE LITTLE PIGS

Words and Music by FRANK CHURCHILL
Additional Lyric by ANN RONELL

A WHOLE NEW WORLD
from Walt Disney's ALADDIN

Music by ALAN MENKEN
Lyrics by TIM RICE

WOODY WOODPECKER

from the Cartoon Television Series

Words and Music by GEORGE TIBBLES
and RAMEY IDRISS

Gm7 C7sus C7 D♭9 C9 F
peck a few holes in your head. Ha ha ha
ha ha, ha ha ha ha ha, that's the
Fmaj7 F6 F♯dim7
8va
Gm7 C7 F6
Wood - y Wood - peck - er's tune. Ha ha ha
F Fmaj7 F6 F♯dim7
ha ha, ha ha ha ha ha, makes the
8va

YELLOW SUBMARINE

from YELLOW SUBMARINE

Words and Music by JOHN LENNON
and PAUL McCARTNEY

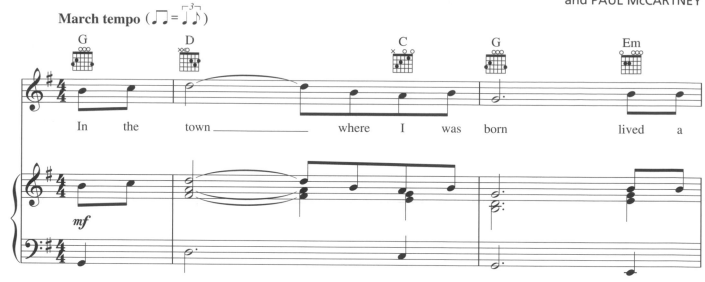

In the town _____ where I was born lived a

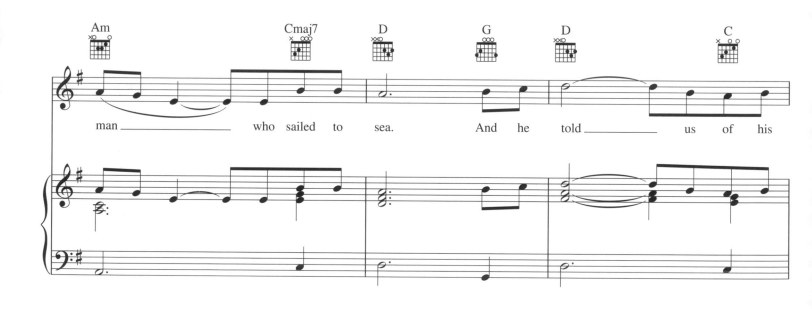

man _____ who sailed to sea. And he told _____ us of his

life in the land _____ of sub-ma-rines. So we

YOU CAN FLY! YOU CAN FLY! YOU CAN FLY!

from Walt Disney's PETER PAN

Words by SAMMY CAHN
Music by SAMMY FAIN

Think of the pres-ents you're brought, an-y mer-ry lit-tle thought.

Think of Christ-mas, think of snow, think of sleigh bells, here we go! Like

rein-deer in the sky. _____ You can fly! You can

YOU'VE GOT A FRIEND IN ME
from Walt Disney's TOY STORY

Music and Lyrics by
RANDY NEWMAN

YOU'LL BE IN MY HEART

(Pop Version)
from Walt Disney Pictures' TARZAN™

Words and Music by
PHIL COLLINS

Come stop your cry - ing; __ it will be all right. Just take my hand,

hold it tight. ___ I will pro-tect you from all a-round __ you.

I will be here; don't you __ cry.

For one so small you
Why can't they un-der-stand the